25

Activities for Teams

With Introductions by Fran Rees

Pfeiffer
& COMPANY

An imprint of
Jossey-Bass Inc., Publishers

Editor: Arlette C. Ballew
Graphic Designer: Heather Kennedy

An imprint of Jossey-Bass Inc., Publishers

350 Sansome Street, Fifth Floor
San Francisco, CA 94104-1342 USA

Orders:
USA (800) 274-4434; FAX (800) 605-2665
Worldwide (415) 433-1767; FAX (415) 433-3144

This book is printed on acid-free, recycled stock that meets or exceeds
the minimum GPO and EPA specifications for recycled paper.

Table of

Contents

Introduction 1

1. Leading Meetings 5
   Ten Characteristics of Effective Meetings. 7
   Creating Agendas: Using a Checklist. 9
   Creating a Checklist for Team Meetings. 13
   Getting Started: Setting the Stage for Team Building. 17
   Meetings Questionnaire: Planning for Improvements. 19
   Postmeeting Reactions Form 21

2. Empowering Participants 23
   Creative Team Building 25
   Imagination: Thinking Creatively 27
   Visual Riddles: Thinking Creatively 29
   Work Motivators 33
   Useful Feedback: Establishing the Process 35
   Collaborating To Identify Problems 39
   Identifying and Improving Listening Habits 45

3. Aiming for Consensus 53
   Brainstorming 55
   Problems and Solutions 61
   The Nominal Group Technique 63
   Communication in Problem Solving: The Shoe Store 67
   Team Blasphemies: Clarifying Values 69

4. Directing the Process and Diagnosis 73
   Task Delegation: A Team Approach 75
   Conflict Management: Developing a Procedure 79
   Leadership Style 83
   Characteristics of Effective Team Members 89
   Characteristics of Effective Team Leaders 93
   Effective Team-Member Assessment 101
   Effective Team-Leader Assessment 103
   Effective Team Assessment 105

   References and Bibliography. 108

Introduction

The move toward greater employee participation has given rise to many kinds of decision-making work teams. Whether they are striving to improve quality, increase efficiency, focus on customer satisfaction, or accommodate a diversity of perspectives, people support what they are involved in. This underlies the participative approach.

The focus on employee participation requires a more facilitative, empowering, and less directive, controlling leadership style. Facilitative leaders learn to use the abilities of their groups to solve problems and make decisions. Being able to develop a team and use the group process to run an effective team meeting are essential skills of the facilitative leader.

This book, *25 Activities for Teams*, is designed to assist team leaders in leading and developing their teams. The book may be used as a companion to the book, *How to LEAD Work Teams*, by Fran Rees. The team leader can use the LEAD model and the activities in this book to Lead with a clear purpose, Empower participants, Aim for consensus, and Direct the process.

The following table illustrates tasks involved in each phase of the LEAD model. The activities in this book are intended to support these tasks, in conjunction with the ideas presented in the Rees book.

This book is meant to be a valuable companion to team leaders and facilitators. Using the activities in this book with actual work teams will help you to develop team skills, build team cohesiveness, and accomplish important team tasks. Specifically, these activities will help your team to:

- Plan and evaluate its meetings, solve problems, resolve team conflicts, and reach consensus.
- Develop and learn important team-member skills.
- Increase team members' understanding of teams and how teams work.
- Improve interpersonal relationships between team members.
- Improve team members' observational skills.
- Encourage creativity in the team.

Leader Functions	Group Needs Met	Leader Tasks	Team-Member Tasks
Lead with a clear purpose	• Common goals • Attention to content • Leadership	• Set boundaries • Interpret company goals • Facilitate team's setting of its goals • Evaluate and track progress toward goals	• Ask questions to test own understanding • Participate in setting goals for team • Help leader track and evaluate progress toward goals
Empower to participate	• High level of involvement of all members • Maintenance of self-esteem • Leadership • Respect for differences • Trust	• Ask questions • Listen • Show understanding • Summarize • Seek divergent viewpoints • Record ideas	• Contribute ideas from own experience and knowledge • Listen to others • Build on others' ideas • Consider others' ideas • Ask questions • Think creatively
Aim for consensus	• Constructive conflict resolution • Power within group to make decisions • Leadership • Trust	• Use group-process techniques (brainstorming, problem solving, prioritization, etc.) • Ask questions • Listen • Seek common interests • Summarize • Confront in a constructive way	• Focus on common interests and goals • Listen to and consider others' ideas • Make own needs known • Disagree in a constructive way
Direct the process	• Attention to process • Leadership • Trust	• Give clear directions • Intervene to keep group on track • Read group and adjust • Remain neutral • Suggest alternate processes to help group achieve goal	• Listen • Keep purpose in mind • Stay focused on objective • Use own energy and enthusiasm to help process along

Using the L.E.A.D. Model

How to use this book

It is suggested that you regularly incorporate these activities into the work and development of your team. There is no prescribed order in which to do them. However, it is helpful for teams to establish some healthy meeting habits early on, because most team work is accomplished in meetings. It also is a good idea to intersperse some of the activities that are fun (as well as productive) into the team's work from time to time.

Reprinted from *How to LEAD Work Teams: Facilitation Skills*, by Fran Rees. Copyright © 1991 by Pfeiffer & Company, San Diego, CA.

Introduction

Tips for leading these activities

To get the most out of these activities:

- Don't rush. Allow plenty of time to experience and discuss the activity.
- Post the goals of the activity for all to see.
- Make sure that you understand the activity and all its steps before attempting to facilitate it.
- When facilitating the activity, remain neutral as much as possible. Try to draw out and record the thoughts and ideas of team members without taking over.
- Strive for a balance of participation among all team members.

To capitalize on the experience of the team activity, it is a good idea to record the key learnings, decisions, and action items that come out of the activity. These then can be reproduced and shared with all team members.

When wrapping up the activity:

- Ask the team members to share any learnings and insights they had from the activity. Record and post these.
- Ask if the team should consider making any changes in the way that it operates as a result of this activity. Record and post any suggestions.
- Ask if there were specific decisions made during the activity that the team must now implement. Record and post these.
- Record and post any action items. Specify **who** will do **what** by **when**.

Activity Wrap-Up

- ☐ Share and post learnings
- ☐ Determine and post any changes
- ☐ Determine and post any decisions
- ☐ Post action items and accountability

Chapter

Leading Meetings

The team leader or facilitator fills an important leadership function by helping the team to conduct successful meetings. Regular, well-managed meetings are critical to a team's success. Team meetings are where most consensus decisions are made and where team issues and goals are reviewed and resolved.

If it is effective, the team meeting can be an energizer and a motivator. If it is ineffective, it can be a drain on energy and it can discourage team efforts. It pays, then, to guide the team members in taking part in designing and contributing productively to team meetings. The goal is for each member to take ownership for the success of the team meetings and for his or her own meeting behaviors. The following activities are designed to help team members to make their meetings successful.

Ten Characteristics of Effective Meetings

1. The seating in the room is arranged so that every person can see everyone else.

2. At the front of the room, equipment is provided to record ideas and decisions. An easel holding a newsprint flip chart (with felt-tipped markers for writing) is preferable, so that the recorded data can be saved. A white board (with special felt-tipped markers) or a chalkboard and chalk can be used, but must be erased after the meeting.

3. An agenda for the meeting is presented, amended, and agreed on.

4. Time estimates are determined for each agenda item.

5. At least once or twice during the meeting, someone asks, "How are we doing in our process today? How can we be more productive?"

6. During the meeting, someone records the ideas generated and the decisions made. These data are prepared in handout form afterward and distributed to all concerned.

7. The meeting notes indicate who has agreed to do what before the next meeting, and by when.

8. Dates of future meetings (not just the next meeting) are set well in advance so that people can make arrangements to attend.

9. Those in attendance consider whether anyone else should be involved in the decisions/future meetings and, if so, who.

10. At the end of the meeting, people review and confirm who will be doing what before the next meeting.

Adapted from E. Schindler-Rainman, R. Lippitt, & J. Cole (1988). *Taking Your Meetings Out of the Doldrums* (rev. ed.). San Diego, CA: Pfeiffer & Company.

Creating Agendas: Using a Checklist

Goals: I. To assist the team members in reviewing an agenda and finding ways to improve it.

II. To assist the team members in redrafting an agenda.

Time: One hour.

Materials: I. A copy of the Sample Agenda for each team member.

II. A copy of the Checklist for each team member.

III. Several sheets of blank paper and a pencil for each team member.

IV. A newsprint flip chart and a felt-tipped marker.

V. Masking tape for posting newsprint.

Setting: A room with a chair and a writing surface for each team member. Each member should be seated so that he or she can see the other team members as well as the leader and the newsprint flip chart.

Procedure: I. The leader introduces the activity by explaining its goals.

II. Each team member is given a copy of the Sample Agenda and is asked to read it and to jot down on the bottom of the sheet seven ways in which the agenda can be improved. (Five minutes.)

III. The leader asks the team members to take turns sharing their suggestions with the rest of the team. The leader records these suggestions on newsprint and posts the newsprint. When two or more members offer the same suggestion, the leader places a tick mark by the original suggestion. (Fifteen minutes.)

IV. Each team member is given a copy of the Checklist, several sheets of blank paper, and a pencil.

V. The leader asks the members to work together to rewrite the agenda in improved form. The leader explains that they should refer to the Checklist

---

Adapted from W.R. Daniels (1986). *Group Power I: A Manager's Guide to Using Task-Force Meetings.* San Diego, CA: Pfeiffer & Company.

and to the suggestions that are posted as they create the new agenda. (Twenty minutes.)

VI. After the team has completed the task, the leader asks one member to read the revised agenda and leads a discussion based on questions such as these:

1. In what ways does the new agenda meet the needs of the people who will attend the meeting?

2. Which items on the Checklist were not addressed? Why?

3. In what ways can you use what you have learned in creating agendas for your own meetings?

The leader records any salient points on newsprint and gives the newsprint to one of the members for subsequent reproduction and distribution to the other members.

Variation: Instead of using the Sample Agenda, the team members may work together to create an agenda for a particular meeting, then work to improve it.

Memo From: Max

Date: June 18

Subject: Monthly staff meeting, June 21

Please be on time!

We have a lot to cover. RE: Summer schedule, and we'd like to get things done quickly.

See you there.

Use this checklist in creating an agenda for an effective meeting.

General Information

_____ Name of team

_____ Title of meeting

_____ Who is calling the meeting

_____ Date

_____ Starting time

_____ Ending time

_____ Place

_____ Agenda put out ahead of meeting (at least one day but not more than one week ahead of time, so it will be fresh in people's minds)

_____ Desired outcomes

_____ Meeting procedure (for example, any of various problem-solving techniques, presentations, discussions)

_____ Decision-making method (for example, voting agreement of all members)

_____ Final decision maker (team, leader, other)

_____ Preparation suggestions (for example, background materials)

_____ Other notes to participants

People Attending

_____ Leader

_____ Team members

_____ Role assignments (for example, subject-matter experts, implementation specialist, recorder, facilitator)

_____ Guest resource people

Agenda Schedule

_____ Sequence of items

_____ Person(s) responsible for each item

_____ Procedure for dealing with each item

_____ Time allocated for each item

Creating a Checklist for Team Meetings

Goals: I. To provide the team members with a checklist for keeping a meeting on target and for tracking their progress.

II. To help the team members to create a meetings checklist that is applicable to their situation.

Time: Approximately one hour.

Materials: I. A copy of the Sample Meetings Checklist for each team member.

II. A few sheets of blank paper and a pencil for each team member.

III. A newsprint flip chart and a felt-tipped marker.

IV. Masking tape for posting newsprint.

Setting: A room with a chair and a writing surface for each team member. Each member should be seated so that he or she can see the other team members as well as the leader and the newsprint flip chart.

Procedure: I. The leader introduces the activity by explaining its goals.

II. Each team member is given a copy of the Sample Meetings Checklist and is asked to read it. Explaining that this sample checklist is used by a real company, the leader reviews each item on the checklist and leads a discussion based on questions such as the following:

1. Why would the items on this checklist be important to a team?

2. How might some of these items be changed to be more applicable to the meetings of this team?

3. What items are missing that would be important to this team?

Salient points are recorded on newsprint and posted. (Fifteen minutes.)

III. If the team consists of more than five members, the leader asks them to work in subgroups of three or four members each. Each team member is given a pencil and a few sheets of paper. Based on the previous discussion, one or

---

Adapted from M. Kitzmiller, "Checkpoints: Creating a Check List for Team Meetings," in J.W. Pfeiffer (Ed.) (1991). *The Encyclopedia of Team-Development Activities.* San Diego, CA: Pfeiffer & Company.

more checklist items are assigned to each subgroup (depending on the number of subgroups). The subgroups work on the assigned items to word them positively, appropriately, and concisely. Each subgroup selects a spokesperson to report later to the total team. (Fifteen minutes.)

IV. After all team members have completed the task, the leader reconvenes the team and asks the spokespersons to take turns sharing their revised items. As the items are read, the leader records them on newsprint and posts the newsprint. (Five minutes.)

V. The leader helps the team members to reach consensus on a checklist they wish to use in their meetings. When the agreed-on checklist has been recorded on newsprint, the leader gives it to one of the members who will prepare a copy for the meeting room and/or for each member of the team. (Five minutes.)

VI. The leader leads a discussion based on questions such as the following:

    1. How will the checklist be used?

    2. At which meetings will the checklist be appropriate?

    3. In what ways will the checklist change our meetings?

(Five minutes.)

VII. The leader models the use of the team's new checklist by reviewing each item in light of the current meeting.

A consensus decision is one that all team members can accept, regardless of how satisfied they are with it. Each member's opinion must be heard; no "majority-rule" voting, bargaining, or averaging is allowed.

1. Follow up the last meeting and recheck action steps.

2. Ask "Who?" and "By when?"

3. Ask "Who else needs to know what happened at this meeting? Who will inform them?"

4. Share responsibility for saying that the meeting is not working.

5. Debrief at the end of the meeting.

Getting Started: Setting the Stage for Team Building

Goals: I. To assist the team members in creating an agenda for a team-building session and in rank ordering the items on that agenda.

II. To generate ownership of and commitment to commonly perceived problems that face the team.

III. To develop the team members' listening skills.

Time: Approximately one hour.

Materials: I. Blank paper and a pencil for each team member.

II. A newsprint flip chart and a felt-tipped marker.

III. Masking tape for posting newsprint.

Setting: A room large enough so that pairs of team members can meet privately without disturbing one another. Writing surfaces and movable chairs should be provided.

Procedure: I. The leader discusses the goals of the activity and gives a brief overview of the design.

II. The team members are given paper and pencils and are instructed to form pairs. The leader stipulates that each team member should select a person with whom he or she has not talked recently.

III. When the pairs have assembled in separate places in the room, the leader tells the partners to take turns interviewing each other on the topic "What problem situations should we work on in our upcoming team-building session?" The leader states that each interview should last five minutes and that the interviewer should make notes on the content of the interview. Then the team members are told to begin.

Adapted from J.E. Jones, "Agenda Setting: A Team-Building Starter," in J.W. Pfeiffer and J.E. Jones (Eds.) (1975). *A Handbook of Structured Experiences for Human Relations Training* (Vol. V). San Diego, CA: Pfeiffer & Company.

IV. After the interviewing phase has been completed, the team is reassembled in a circle. The members take turns reporting what their partners said, and the leader lists on newsprint each member's suggested problem situations (in the member's own words). Each member whose comments appear on newsprint then adds anything that the interviewer left out and/or corrects any misperceptions. During this phase, the team member's are told that they may respond only by asking questions for clarification.

V. The lists of problem situations are posted, and the items are numbered. Duplicates are combined or are given the same number.

VI. The leader instructs each team member to select, by number, the three problem situations that he or she believes are most important. Then the leader tallies on the newsprint the number of members who have indicated each of the items.

VII. The leader posts a new list of the items with the highest frequencies in the tally.

VIII. Each team member is instructed to rank order these problem situations independently, in terms of which are most important. The rank of 1 is to be assigned to the item that the member believes must be discussed if the team-building session is to be successful. The second-most-important situation is to be ranked 2, and so on.

IX. The leader tallies the ranks assigned to the items by asking how many members ranked each item as 1, 2, 3, and so on. (If there are more than six or seven items, the tally may be based on a ranking of high, medium, or low.)

X. The leader posts the final agenda on newsprint and then leads a discussion of reactions to the agenda-setting process.

Variation: If the team-building session is to be held immediately after this activity, the interview time may be varied as necessary. If the agenda-setting time is limited, the interviewers may ask for the one problem situation that needs to be faced by the team.

Meetings Questionnaire: Planning for Improvements

Goals: I. To present some criteria by which team meetings can be assessed.

II. To explore the team members' perceptions of the planning and process of their team meetings.

III. To provide an opportunity for the team members to develop plans to improve their meetings.

Time: A minimum of one hour.

Materials: I. A copy of the Meetings Questionnaire and a pencil for each team member.

II. A newsprint flip chart and felt-tipped markers.

III. Masking tape for posting newsprint.

Procedure: I. The leader distributes the Meetings Questionnaire and pencils to the team members and asks them to read the instructions on the questionnaire and to respond to each item.

II. After the members have completed their questionnaires, the team members decide whether to report their scores anonymously or orally.

III. The leader charts the rank order of the headings on newsprint, placing those having the highest scores at the top.

IV. The team selects the statement with the highest single score and agrees on specific actions that can be taken to overcome the problem at the next meeting.

V. This process is continued at successive meetings so that each problem can be worked through in descending order.

Variation: The Postmeeting Reactions Form may be used in lieu of the Meetings Questionnaire.

Adapted from D. Francis and D. Young, "How Good Are Your Meetings?" (1979). *Improving Work Groups: A Practical Manual for Team Building.* San Diego, CA: Pfeiffer & Company.

Instructions: Read the three scored headings and use them to evaluate each statement that follows. Choose one score (4, 2, or 0) that corresponds to your opinion of how the statement applies to your team's meetings. Write the score in the appropriate blank.

	True (Usually) 4	Sometimes 2	Not True (Seldom) 0
1. The purposes of our meetings are not defined.	——	——	——
2. We do not decide what we want to achieve by the end of a meeting.	——	——	——
3. People do not prepare sufficiently for our meetings.	——	——	——
4. We seldom review our progress during meetings.	——	——	——
5. We do not allocate meeting time well.	——	——	——
6. Ideas and views often are lost or forgotten.	——	——	——
7. We do not decide which agenda items have priority.	——	——	——
8. We allocate equal amounts of time to trivia and important issues.	——	——	——
9. We often are diverted from the matter at hand.	——	——	——
10. People lose concentration and attention.	——	——	——
11. Sometimes there are several meetings when there should be one.	——	——	——
12. We do not review and confirmwhat has been agreed on and how those decisions will be activated.	——	——	——

Instructions: Circle the number on each scale that most nearly represents your opinion.

1. How well did we do today in accomplishing our task?

Task Accomplishment

1	2	3	4	5
Poor	Fair	Satisfactory	Good	Excellent

Suggestions for improving task accomplishment:

2. How well did we do today in working as a team and building our relationships?

Team Cohesiveness

1	2	3	4	5
Poor	Fair	Satisfactory	Good	Excellent

Suggestions for improving team cohesiveness:

Adapted from H.G. Dimock (1987). *Groups: Leadership and Group Development.* San Diego, CA: Pfeiffer & Company.

3. How clear were we about our goals?

Clarity of Goals

1	2	3	4	5
Confused	Unclear	Fairly Clear	Clear	Very Clear

Suggestions for improving clarity of team goals:

4. How cooperatively did we work?

Team Cooperation

1	2	3	4	5
Uncooperatively	Independently	Somewhat Cooperatively	Cooperatively	As a Real Team

Suggestions for improving team cooperation:

5. How productive were we?

Team Productivity

1	2	3	4	5
Unproductive	Not Truly Productive	Somewhat Productive	Productive	Very Productive

Suggestions for improving team productivity:

Chapter 2

Empowering Participants

The following activities will help you to encourage productive and creative involvement from all team members. As you lead these activities, remember that you are serving as the *facilitator,* thus, your key role is to help the team to solve its *own* problems. Your role is to clarify the process, ask questions, listen, show interest and understanding, seek divergent viewpoints, record ideas, and summarize.

You also will need to gently encourage team members to listen actively to one another, consider the ideas and feelings of others, not be judgmental, contribute their own ideas freely and creatively, ask questions, and build on the ideas of others.

Creative Team Building

Goal: To provide the team members with experience in creating a team-building activity.

Group Size: Ten to twenty participants.

Time: Approximately one-half hour.

Setting: An unobstructed area, without tables or chairs, that is large enough to permit the unrestricted movement of the participants. Several small meeting rooms or areas that provide private or semiprivate interaction also are needed.

Procedure:

I. The leader begins by dividing the total team into work groups of four or five members each (depending on the size of the total group).

II. When the groups have been formed, the leader explains that the group members will be taking part in an activity that will challenge their creativity. Each work group is to create an exercise or game that the work group's members believe will promote or build group spirit.

III. After explaining that the game or exercise should be planned to involve all team members and should be less than five minutes in length, the leader tells each work group to find an area in which it can work with some degree of privacy. The work groups have ten minutes in which to devise their creative, team-building activities.

IV. When the allotted time has elapsed, the leader calls the work groups together. Each work group then leads the entire group in its team-building game or exercise.

V. After all the work groups have presented their activities, the leader may process the experience through a discussion of the types of activities, attitudes, and behaviors that promote cooperative efforts in the work environment.

Adapted from S. Forbess-Greene (1983). *The Encyclopedia of Icebreakers: Structured Activities that Warm-Up, Motivate, Challenge, Acquaint and Energize.* San Diego, CA: Pfeiffer & Company.

Imagination: Thinking Creatively

Goal: To encourage the team members to think creatively as they respond to unusual questions.

Group Size: Unlimited, but best with a group of ten to twenty participants.

Time: Five to ten minutes.

Materials: For the leader, a copy of the Imagination List.

Setting: A room in which the participants can be seated comfortably.

Procedure: I. The leader asks the group members to let their minds expand in order to allow for innovative ways of thinking and perceiving.

II. Next, the leader explains that in this activity the team members will be asked to respond to some questions and then to explain why they responded as they did.

III. The leader chooses a team member at random and asks him or her a question from the Imagination List. When the group member has given his or her response and has provided a rationale for it, the leader may ask another member to answer the same question or a different question from the Imagination List. This is continued until each member of the team has responded to at least one question.

IV. The leader initiates a processing discussion in terms of the activity's relevance to problem solving, brainstorming, or the examination of basic assumptions.

Adapted from S. Forbess-Greene (1983). *The Encyclopedia of Icebreakers: Structured Activities that Warm-Up, Motivate, Challenge, Acquaint and Energize.* San Diego, CA: Pfeiffer & Company.

1. What shape is a wish?

2. What does happiness look like?

3. What color is today?

4. What does purple taste like?

5. What does your self-image sound like?

6. What does a rainbow feel like?

7. What color is the smell of your favorite perfume?

8. What is the distance of your life?

9. What is your favorite sense?

10. What color is your favorite song?

11. What texture is your favorite scent?

12. What does inspiration taste like?

13. What is the shape of violin music?

14. What is the texture of the letter "P"?

15. What is the texture of a whisper?

16. What color is the fragrance of soap?

17. What does a cloud sound like?

18. What is the weight of your anger?

19. What is the shape of your imagination?

20. What does your favorite book feel like?

Visual Riddles: Thinking Creatively

Goal: To have team members to think creatively as they attempt to solve a series of visual riddles.

Time: Five to ten minutes.

Materials: I. A copy of the Riddles List for the leader.

II. A newsprint flip chart and felt-tipped marker.

Setting: A room in which the participants can be seated comfortably.

Procedure: I. The leader explains that the team members will be asked to think creatively in order to solve a series of visual riddles.

II. The leader then tells the team members that they will be shown a series of diagrams (see Riddles List) one at a time and that they will have three minutes in which to determine what each one means. The group members may ask any questions they wish, but the leader can only answer "yes" or "no."

III. The leader draws the first diagram on the newsprint. The group members may ask questions as they attempt to guess the meaning of the riddle.

IV. If the correct answer has not been guessed after three minutes, the leader announces it. He or she then draws the second diagram, and the team members attempt to guess its meaning. This process continues until the members have viewed and then attempted to decipher all of the visual riddles.

V. The leader may process the activity by means of a discussion of the elements of creative thinking, primarily the ability to view a situation from a different or new perspective.

Adapted from S. Forbess-Greene, "Entrance Exams" (1983). *The Encyclopedia of Icebreakers: Structured Activities that Warm-Up, Motivate, Challenge, Acquaint and Energize.* San Diego, CA: Pfeiffer & Company.

Variations: I. The leader may instruct the members to work individually to solve the riddles.

II. The leader may ask the members to devise their own visual riddles for the rest of the group members to solve.

1. O
    ———
    Ph.D.
    M.A.
    B.S.

2. (C L O U S E R B) *arranged in circle*

3. LE
    VEL

4.   J
    YOU U ME
        S
        T

5. W
    O
    R
    H
    T

6. T
    O
    W
    N

7. R
    E
    T
    T
    A
    B

8. HE'S HIMSELF

9. CRAZY
    ———
    YOU

10. OATH
    ———
    UR

Answers:

1. Three degrees below zero

2. See-through blouse

3. Split level

4. Just between you and me

5. Throw up

6. Downtown

7. Batter up

8. He's beside himself

9. Crazy over you

10. You are under oath

Work Motivators

Goal: To provide an opportunity for the team members to identify and examine the motivating qualities in their work environment.

Group Size: Ten or more participants.

Time: Fifteen to thirty minutes.

Materials: For each team member, a pencil and a 5" x 7" index card that is marked off into nine sections and labeled to accord with the Completed Sample Grid Card. The cards should be prepared by the leader before the activity begins.

Setting: A room that has the potential for flexible seating.

Procedure: I. The leader tells the group members that during this activity, each team member will be identifying and then examining the qualities of his or her work environment that motivate him or her to perform more effectively and/or more efficiently.

II. After giving each team member a pencil and a Grid Card, the leader explains that, in each section of the card, the member is to list a factor or quality that **motivates** him or her to accomplish assigned tasks competently and/or to further his or her professional expertise.

III. After five minutes, the leader asks the team members to form pairs and then to exchange cards with their partners. (If the total group contains an uneven number of members, one subgroup of three may be formed.) After reading his or her partner's card, each member places a check mark beside each item that the partners have in common.

IV. The partners are directed to take back their own cards and to discuss the factors that motivate them.

V. The leader processes the activity by having all partners share with the entire group the listed items that they have in common and any salient points from their discussions.

VI. If time allows, the leader may initiate a discussion of what motivates people in the workplace, why there may be differences among people, and what groups/organizations can do to try to motivate as many workers as possible.

Adapted from S. Forbess-Greene (1983). *The Encyclopedia of Icebreakers: Structured Activities that Warm-Up, Motivate, Challenge, Acquaint and Energize.* San Diego, CA: Pfeiffer & Company.

Salary	**Benefits**	**Vacation Time**
Comfortable Work Environment	**Job Responsibilities**	**Enjoyable Co-Workers**
Status of Position	**Power**	**Attention from Others**

Useful Feedback: Establishing the Process

Goal: To help the team members to establish their own guidelines for giving and receiving personal feedback.

Time: One hour to one hour and fifteen minutes.

Materials: I. A copy of the Characteristics of Useful Feedback handout for each team member.

II. A copy of the Ranking Sheet for each team member.

III. A pencil for each team member.

IV. A newsprint flip chart and a felt-tipped marker.

V. Masking tape for posting newsprint.

Setting: A room with a table and chairs for the team members. If a table is not available, the leader may substitute clipboards or other portable writing surfaces. Plenty of wall space should be available for posting newsprint.

Procedure: I. The leader gives a copy of the Characteristics of Useful Feedback handout, a copy of the Ranking Sheet, and a pencil to each team member.

II. Each member is instructed to read the characteristics handout and then to complete the Ranking Sheet by choosing five characteristics from the handout that he or she believes are most significant, listing these in order according to their importance, and writing statements explaining why the chosen characteristics are important. (Fifteen to twenty minutes.)

III. The leader asks the members to take turns presenting their chosen characteristics and explaining briefly why each is important. As each member shares this information, the leader records it on newsprint. Each newsprint sheet is posted after it is filled. (Fifteen minutes.)

Adapted from D. Francis and D. Young (1979). *Improving Work Groups: A Practical Manual for Team Building.* San Diego, CA: Pfeiffer & Company.

A consensus decision is one that all team members can accept, regardless of how satisfied they are with it. Each member's opinion must be heard; no "majority-rule" voting, bargaining, or averaging is allowed.

IV. The leader reviews the posted information with the members and assists them in achieving consensus about the following:

1. Which feedback characteristics they want to use as guidelines for their own team;

2. Which they would like to omit, if any; and

3. The order of importance of the retained characteristics.

V. When the members have agreed about the guidelines for giving and receiving feedback in their team and the order of importance of these guidelines, the leader records the final, numbered guidelines on newsprint and writes these words at the top of the list: *For this team, useful feedback is:....* Then the leader gives the newsprint list to a volunteer to reproduce and distribute to all team members. The leader also suggests posting a copy in the room where the team usually holds its meetings. (Ten minutes.)

V. Before adjourning, the leader elicits reactions to the activity and then makes appropriate concluding comments.

Characteristics of Useful Feedback

Useful feedback is:

1. *Given with care.* To be useful, feedback requires the giver to feel concern for the person receiving the feedback—to want to help rather than hurt the recipient.

2. *Given with attention.* It is important for the giver to pay attention to what he or she is doing while giving feedback. This promotes a two-way exchange with some depth of communication.

3. *Invited by the recipient.* Feedback is most effective when the recipient has invited the comments. This provides a platform for openness and some guidelines; it also gives the recipient an opportunity to identify and explore particular areas of concern.

4. *Expressed directly.* Good feedback is specific; it clearly describes observable behavior and specific incidents. Making general or vague comments about an issue is of little value. The most useful feedback is direct, open, and concrete.

5. *Expressed fully.* Effective feedback requires more than a bald statement of facts. Feeling reactions also need to be expressed so that the recipient can judge the full impact of his or her behavior.

6. *Uncluttered by evaluative judgments.* Feedback is most helpful when it does not consist of judgments or evaluations, such as assuming the other person's motivations or intentions. If judgments must be included, the giver should first state clearly that these are matters of subjective evaluation, then describe the situation as he or she sees it, and, finally, let the recipient make the evaluation.

7. *Well-timed.* The most useful feedback is given when the recipient is receptive to it and is sufficiently close to the particular event being discussed for it to be fresh in his or her mind. Storing comments over time can lead to a buildup of recriminations that reduces the effectiveness of the feedback when it is finally given.

8. *Easily acted on.* The most useful feedback deals with behavior that can be changed by the recipient. Feedback concerning matters outside the recipient's control is not often useful. Often it is helpful to suggest alternative ways of behaving that allow the recipient to think about new ways of tackling old problems.

9. *Checked and clarified.* If possible, the recipient of the feedback should check with other people to determine whether the giver's perceptions are shared by others. Different viewpoints can be collected and assimilated, points of difference and similarity clarified, and a more objective picture developed.

Ranking Sheet

Characteristic	Why I Think It Is Important
1.	
2.	
3.	
4.	
5.	

Collaborating To Identify Problems

Goals: I. To introduce a process that a team can use to identify and select work-related problems as projects.

    II. To allow the team members to practice behaviors that are associated with effective teamwork: participating collaboratively, listening to other team members, and withholding judgment while considering issues that are before the team.

Time: Approximately one and one-half hours.

Materials: I. A copy of the Work Sheet for each team member.

    II. A copy of the Procedure Sheet for each team member.

    III. A pencil for each team member.

    IV. A newsprint flip chart and a felt-tipped marker.

    V. Masking tape for posting newsprint.

Setting: A room with a chair and a writing surface for each team member.

Procedure: I. The leader introduces the activity as offering a process whereby the team members can identify and select work-related problems as projects.

    II. Each team member is given a copy of the Work Sheet and a pencil and is instructed to complete the sheet. (Ten minutes.)

    III. The team members are instructed to share their Work Sheets with one another and to select the one problem of those listed that they would most like to solve as a team project. As they work on this step, the leader records highlights on newsprint. (Fifteen minutes.)

    IV. The leader distributes copies of the Procedure Sheet and asks the team members to read this sheet. (Five minutes.)

    V. The leader briefly discusses the content of the Procedure Sheet and elicits and answers any questions that the team members may have. The team members are told that although it will not be possible within the course of

Adapted from M.J. Miller, "Project Selection," in J.W. Pfeiffer and L.D. Goodstein (Eds.) (1984). *The 1984 Annual: Developing Human Resources.* San Diego, CA: Pfeiffer & Company.

the activity to complete the entire problem-solving procedure, the time remaining will be spent on the first two steps described in the handout. (Ten minutes.)

    VI. The team is instructed to repeat the process of selecting one work-related problem as a project, but this time the members are to take a different approach and follow Step 1 and Step 2 of the procedure described. The leader emphasizes that the members should practice the behaviors cited in the Procedure Sheet: collaborative participation, careful and thoughtful listening, and withholding judgment until it is time to make a final decision. (Twenty minutes.)

    VII. After the team has chosen a problem as a project, the leader processes the activity by asking questions such as the following:

1. What were the differences in the two procedures that were used to complete the task?

2. Which of these two procedures proved to be more satisfying to you?

3. Did the chosen problem change as a result of the second procedure? If so, how?

4. What appear to be the advantages of the process described in the Procedure Sheet? What are the disadvantages?

5. What additional behaviors (other than those listed in the Procedure Sheet) might be useful to the team as it addresses work-related problems?

6. In your experience, how and by whom are work-related problems usually solved? What is your general level of satisfaction with the outcome? What steps could you personally take to increase your level of satisfaction with the team's problem-solving process and the outcomes of that process?

Variations: I. During Step IV, the leader may lead a discussion by eliciting the team members' feelings about and satisfaction with the first procedure chosen to complete the task.

  II. The activity may be continued by asking the team to complete additional steps of the problem-solving process, as described in the Procedure Sheet.

See also the activity entitled "Brainstorming."

Work Sheet

Instructions: In the spaces provided below, list the **work-related problems** that currently are plaguing your team. Think of a problem as a situation or condition for which you can identify a difference between how things are and how you would like them to be. Be as specific as possible in stating each problem.

1.

2.

3.

4.

5.

Many teams hold meetings for the particular purpose of identifying, analyzing, and solving problems related to their work and work area. They develop recommendations for solving these problems, present their recommendations to management (if necessary), implement solutions, and then evaluate the impact of the implemented solutions.

In order to function effectively, the members of such work teams must develop certain behaviors that allow them to complete the problem-solving procedure. These behaviors include not only participating collaboratively in the team's problem-solving efforts, but also listening carefully to fellow members and withholding judgment about various ideas and suggestions until it is time to select a final solution.

The problem-solving procedure that calls for the use of these behaviors includes the following steps:

1. *Identifying problems.* To identify work-related problems, the team members use a technique called "brainstorming" in which they take turns suggesting problems that might make worthwhile projects. When used effectively, brainstorming works in the following way:

- As ideas are contributed, they are listed on newsprint or a chalkboard.
- Each member offers only one idea per turn. If a member does not have a contribution to make on any particular turn, he or she simply says "pass."
- No opinions about ideas, either positive or negative, may be stated. The withholding of judgment at this point is important so that creativity is not stifled.
- The process continues (if necessary, for several rounds) until all contributions have been exhausted.

2. *Selecting a problem.* A team works on solving only one problem at a time. The members discuss all problems identified in Step 1 and then choose one. The process used to arrive at this choice is governed by the following principles:

- No voting, bargaining, or "horse trading" is permissible.
- Each member must be offered an opportunity to express his or her opinion and the reasons for holding this opinion.
- No member may say that the opinions of another member are "wrong."
- All members must care about the problem that is finally chosen; they must be willing to commit themselves to its resolution.

Adapted from R.G. James and A.J. Elkins (1983). *How to Train and Lead a Quality Circle.* San Diego, CA: Pfeiffer & Company. Also adapted from L. Fitzgerald and J. Murphy (1982). *Installing Quality Circles: A Strategic Approach.* San Diego, CA: Pfeiffer & Company.

Empowering Participants

The members must be able to do something about the chosen problem. Problems that the team cannot possibly solve either on its own or with help provided by management constitute inappropriate projects.

3. *Analyzing the problem.* After a problem has been selected, it must be defined in writing in precise, detailed terms. Defining includes specifying why the situation or condition is a problem; where and when the problem exists; and the impact of the problem on productivity, morale, and so forth. Another task to be completed is determining the causes of the problem, which may necessitate obtaining data from experts.

4. *Generating and evaluating possible solutions.* During this step, the team members think as creatively as possible to come up with a wide range of possible solutions. Brainstorming is the technique that generally is used for this process. Subsequently, the benefits, costs, and possible ramifications of each possibility are considered.

5. *Selecting a solution.* After each possible solution has been analyzed, the team members choose the one that seems most appropriate.

6. *Implementing the solution.* A detailed plan to guide the implementation is essential. When developing this plan, the team members outline what should be done, when the work should begin, and who should do it. They also consider potential new problems and ways to deal with these problems. Finally, they develop a plan for evaluating the solution by determining what they will accept as evidence that the solution has worked, how they will collect and display this evidence, who will collect it, and when it will be collected.

Identifying and Improving Listening Habits

Goals:
I. To help team members to identify their poor listening habits.

II. To allow team members to practice effective listening skills.

Group Size: Any number of pairs.

Time: Approximately one and one-half hours.

Materials:
I. Enough copies of the ABC Listening Sheet for half the team members.

II. Enough copies of the NL Sheet for half the team members.

III. One copy of the Poor Listening Habits handout for each team member.

IV. One copy of the Effective Listening handout for each team member.

V. A pencil for each team member.

VI. A writing surface for each team member.

VII. A newsprint flip chart and a felt-tipped marker.

VIII. Masking tape for posting newsprint.

Setting: A room that is large enough to allow all the pairs to converse without disturbing one another.

Process:
I. The leader explains the goals of the activity and tells the team members that they will be involved in several activities that will require them to exaggerate poor listening habits.

II. The group is divided into pairs.

III. A copy of the ABC Listening Sheet and a pencil are distributed to **one** person in each pair. Each member who does not have an ABC listening sheet is designated "speaker number one" and is instructed to start talking to his or her partner about any subject. (Five minutes.)

IV. The leader stops the conversations and asks how it felt to be the speaker. The leader explains that the listeners were asked to count the speakers'

Adapted from J. Seltzer and L. Howe, "Poor Listening Habits: Identifying and Improving Them," in J.W. Pfeiffer (Ed.) (1987). *The 1987 Annual: Developing Human Resources*. San Diego, CA: Pfeiffer & Company.

words that began with "a," "b," and "c." The listeners are asked, "How did this scorekeeping affect your ability to listen?" (Five minutes.)

V. A copy of the NL Sheet and a pencil are distributed to each number-one speaker, and the other members are designated "speakers number-two." Each speaker number two is instructed to start talking to his or her partner about any subject that is different from the subject that his or her partner chose previously. (Five minutes.)

VI. The leader interrupts the conversation and asks the number-two speakers how it felt to be the speaker. The leader explains that the listeners were instructed not to listen. The number-one speakers are asked what methods they used to keep from listening. The also are asked to recall some of the things that the number-two speakers said. (Five minutes.)

VII. The leader initiates a discussion of which methods of not listening seem to interfere most with listening and how a habit of using such methods can be broken. (Five minutes.)

VIII. The leader gives the following instructions: The number-one speakers will try to talk to their partners about the topics they chose previously, and the number-two speakers will respond by talking about the topics that they chose previously. The pairs are told to continue these conversations until they are told to stop.

IX. After two minutes, the leader interrupts the conversations and asks, "What was the biggest listening problem with these conversations?"

X. The leader announces that the number-one speakers should select new topics and that as they talk, the number-two speakers should interrupt by asking "why" questions (e.g., "Why did he do that?" or "Why is that important?"). The number-one speakers must begin their responses with the word "because."

XI. After two or so minutes, the leader interrupts the conversations and asks, "What were the listening problems in this why-because conversation?"

XII. The leader asks the number-two speakers to choose topics about which they feel positively and strongly. The leader then announces that each number-one speaker will attempt to argue forcefully against the number-two speaker's position.

XIII. After two minutes, the leader asks the members how this conversation felt and what the listening problems were.

XIV. The total group is reassembled. Each team member is given a copy of the Poor Listening Habits handout and a copy of the Effective Listening handout and is asked to read both handouts and to identify his or her own poor listening habits.

XV. The leader elicits comparisons between the items listed on the Poor Listening Habits handout and the listening methods that were used in each of the activities. The members' responses are recorded on newsprint. (Ten minutes.)

XVI. The leader generates a discussion of how to break each poor listening habit and how to acquire the effective listening skills listed on the second handout. (Ten minutes.)

XVII. The members are instructed to resume conversations with their partners. This time, one member of each pair is to relate a personal experience while his or her partner attempts to use effective listening skills.

XVIII. After about two and one-half minutes the leader stops the conversations and tells the members of the pairs to reverse roles. The second member now will talk while the first member will attempt to practice good listening habits. (Two and one-half minutes.)

XIX. The leader guides a discussion of the following questions:

1. How did it feel to be a speaker this time? A listener?

2. How was this last experience similar to and different from the previous experiences in this activity? What poor listening skills did you continue to use?

3. How can you improve your listening skills? With whom do you need to practice more effective listening?

4. What can you conclude about effective listening and its benefits?

(Five minutes.)

Variations: I. The activity can be used as an icebreaker by rotating partners for each conversation.

II. Subgroups can be formed to identify and discuss poor listening habits.

III. The activity can be shortened by eliminating some of the conversations.

Do not allow your partner to read this sheet.

As your partner is talking, keep track of the total number of words that he or she uses that begin with "a," "b," and "c." Do not count the articles "a" and "an," and do not count the conjunction "and." Do **not** tell your partner what you are doing. You can take part in the conversation, but be sure to keep an accurate score while your partner is talking.

A   B   C

Do not allow your partner to read this sheet.

The "NL" in the title stands for "Not Listening." While your partner is talking, your task is to **not listen**. You may attempt to not listen in any way you like, as long as you stay in your seat. You may say something occasionally, but it need not relate to what your partner has been saying. Although your partner may realize that you are not being attentive, do not tell him or her that you are deliberately not listening.

Poor Listening Habits

Most people spend more time listening than they spend on any other communication activity, yet a large percentage of people never learn to listen well. One reason is that they develop **poor** listening habits that continue with them throughout life. The following list contains some of the most common poor listening habits.

1. *Not Paying Attention.* Listeners may allow themselves to be distracted or to think of something else. Also, not wanting to listen often contributes to lack of attention.

2. *"Pseudolistening."* Often, people who are thinking about something else deliberately try to look as though they are listening. Such pretense may leave the speaker with the impression that the listener has heard some important information or instructions offered by the speaker when this is not really true.

3. *Listening but Not Hearing.* Sometimes a person listens only to facts or details or to the way in which they are presented and misses the real meaning of the communication.

4. *Rehearsing.* Some people listen until they want to say something; then they stop listening, start rehearsing what they will say, and wait for an opportunity to respond.

5. *Interrupting.* The listener does not wait until the complete meaning can be determined, but interrupts so forcefully that the speaker stops in mid-sentence.

6. *Hearing What Is Expected.* People frequently think that they heard speakers say what they **expected** them to say. Alternatively, they refuse to hear what they do not want to hear.

7. *Feeling Defensive.* The listeners assume that they know the speaker's intention or why something was said, or for various other reasons, they expect to be attacked.

8. *Listening for a Point of Disagreement.* Some listeners seem to wait for the chance to attack someone. They listen intently for points on which they can disagree.

One way in which people can improve their listening is to identify their own poor listening habits and make an effort to change them. The list on the Poor Listening Habits handout will help people to identify some of their own listening patterns. If the listeners will then pay special attention to the circumstances that seem to invite such behavior, they can consciously attempt to change their habits. For example, if a person realizes that he or she is "pseudolistening" to his or her spouse, the person can ask the spouse to repeat his or her last idea. The person even can say, "I'm sorry; my mind was wandering." The more people become conscious of their listening behaviors, the more likely they are to change their poor listening habits.

Besides ridding themselves of **bad** listening habits, people can acquire **positive** listening habits. Listed below are a few descriptions of behaviors that can lead to effective listening.

1. *Paying Attention.* If people really want to be good listeners, they must, on occasion, force themselves to pay attention to the speakers. When speakers are dull conversationalists, a listener sometimes must use effort to keep from being distracted by other things. It is important not only to focus on the speakers, but to use nonverbal cues (such as eye contact, head nods, and smiles) to let the speakers know that they are being heard.

2. *Listening for the Whole Message.* This includes looking for meaning and consistency or congruence in both the verbal and nonverbal messages and listening for ideas, feelings, and intentions as well as facts. It also includes hearing things that are unpleasant or unwelcome.

3. *Hearing Before Evaluating.* Listening to what someone says without drawing premature conclusions is a valuable aid to listening. By questioning the speaker in a nonaccusing manner, rather than giving advice or judging, a listener often can discover exactly what the speaker has in mind—which many times is quite different from what the listener had assumed.

4. *Paraphrasing What Was Heard.* If the listener nonjudgmentally paraphrases the words of the speaker and asks if that is what was meant, many misunderstandings and misinterpretations can be avoided.

Chapter 3

Aiming for Consensus

The purpose of these activities is to help your team experience different methods of reaching consensus. Team members frequently are confused about consensus. They may think it means that everyone must end up agreeing with everyone else. They may be apprehensive about being expected to achieve consensus, especially on topics and issues of long-standing concern and disagreement.

It will help to share the following points with team members as you lead the consensus activities.

1. Consensus is not 100 percent agreement. Consensus is when everyone can fully support a team decision. It is a win-win solution in which everyone feels that the best solution has been reached, and no one had to give in on any strongly held convictions or needs.

2. Reaching consensus takes time. It often means finding a new solution that no one has thought of before—one that will serve everyone's greatest needs.

3. Because it takes time and energy to achieve consensus, it should be reserved for important decisions that require a high degree of support from those who will implement them.

4. Less-important decisions can be delegated to a subgroup, to an individual team member, or to the team leader. (Make sure that team members are not absolving themselves of responsibility or difficulty by simply letting someone else make the decision. Team members must fully support the decisions they delegate to someone else.)

5. Teams sometimes try so hard to achieve harmony and quick, efficient consensus that they fall into the bad habit of Groupthink—the tendency for team members to place a high priority on agreeing with one another. This discourages questioning and divergent thinking, hinders creativity, and usually leads to an inferior decision. Members should attempt to explore alternatives.

Brainstorming

Goals: I. To allow the team members to learn about the technique of brainstorming.

II. To offer the team members an opportunity to practice brainstorming.

II. To encourage the team members to use a proven technique to solve a group problem.

Group Size: Twelve to twenty participants in groups of four or five members each.

Time: Approximately one hour.

Setting: A room with movable chairs.

Materials: I. A copy of the Procedure and Rules for Brainstorming for each team member.

II. A copy of the Madison Avenue Problem for each team member.

III. Blank paper and a pencil for each team member.

IV. A newsprint flip chart and a felt-tipped marker for each group.

V. Masking tape for posting newsprint, for each group.

Procedure: I. The leader tells the team members that in this activity they will use the technique of "brainstorming" to do individual and then group problem solving. The leader distributes copies of the Procedure and Rules for Brainstorming, tells the members to read it, and elicits and answers any questions about the brainstorming procedure. (Ten minutes.)

II. The leader gives each member a copy of the Madison Avenue Problem, a sheet of blank paper, and a pencil. Working individually, each member then spends ten minutes brainstorming as many possible solutions as he or she can and recording these solutions on his or her sheet of paper.

III. After ten minutes, the leader calls time and asks the members to hold on to their lists of ideas. The leader then directs them to form groups of four persons each. (There may be a group of five if there is an odd number of participants).

Adapted from S. Forbess-Greene (1983). *The Encyclopedia of Icebreakers: Structured Activities that Warm-Up, Motivate, Challenge, Acquaint and Energize.* San Diego, CA: Pfeiffer & Company. Also adapted from J.W. Pfeiffer and J.E. Jones (Eds.) (1974). *A Handbook of Structured Experiences for Human Relations Training* (Vol. III, rev.). San Diego, CA: Pfeiffer & Company. Also adapted from J.W. Pfeiffer (Ed.) and A.C. Ballew (Assoc. Ed.) (1991). *Theories and Models in Applied Behavioral Science* (Vol. 3: Management/Leadership). San Diego, CA: Pfeiffer & Company.

IV. The groups are given newsprint, felt-tipped markers, and masking tape and are directed to spend five minutes brainstorming additional solutions to the same problem and recording them on the newsprint, reproducing the original phrasing as closely as possible.

V. The leader reassembles the total group and asks the team members how they felt about the individual versus the group brainstorming process.

VI. The leader asks the members to compare the number of solutions generated in the individual and in the group problem-solving efforts.

VII. The leader then asks, "Do you think there were more solutions generated in the group session solely because there were more people or was there some other factor at work?" When the members have responded, the leader then tells the group that the concept of synergy says that the whole is more than the sum of its parts; that is, people often build on the ideas of others, so working with others can spark ideas and creativity that often do not occur when one is working alone. This is why combinations of, additions to, and variations of ideas are encouraged in brainstorming sessions.

VIII. The leader tells the members that they will now engage in the second half of the activity. The leader helps them to establish criteria for evaluating their ideas. These criteria are written on newsprint and posted prominently so that all members can see them throughout the evaluation phase. (Ten minutes.)

IX. The groups are reformed, and the members discuss and evaluate their ideas and select the most workable single idea or combination of ideas. (Fifteen minutes.)

X. The total group is assembled, and the leader leads a discussion of the activity, eliciting the members' ideas about how they can use the technique to their best advantage in future problem-solving efforts.

Variations:
I. Another possible problem is that each team member is to imagine being cast ashore on a deserted island, nude, and with nothing but a belt (flashlight, rope, oar, or corkscrew). The problem is to figure out what can be done with the belt (or alternative object). The leader tells the members that they have fifteen minutes to generate ideas and asks them to begin.

II. Two different problems may be presented; one for the individual process and a new one for the group process.

III. After Step IX, the groups may be asked to share their solutions to the problem.

IV. If appropriate, a real problem that is facing the group may be used in place of or following the problem presented in the procedure.

The Idea-Generation Phase

1. The team members sit so that they can see one another and the newsprint flip chart.

2. The brainstorming session begins with a statement of the problem or topic in specific terms. The problem should be simple, rather than complex, so that the group can focus on a single target.

3. One idea about how to solve the problem is offered by any one member. Then, the individual to that person's left (or right) contributes an idea, and so on around the group until no one has any ideas left. Only one member speaks at a time. This allows all members the "space" to participate and encourages "piggybacking" on previous ideas.

4. While the members are contributing ideas, a recorder (not necessarily the leader) lists all ideas (but not who suggested them) on newsprint or a chalk board as soon as the ideas are generated. The exact wording of each idea is duplicated as closely as possible.

5. The list of ideas is positioned so that all members can see it all the time.

6. Anyone may "pass" on a particular round if he or she has nothing to contribute.

7. The time allotted for idea generation may be from a portion of an hour (intensive brainstorming) to several days ("add new ideas as you think of them"), depending on the needs and schedule of the group.

Rules:

a. No criticism, evaluation, judgment, or defense of ideas is to occur during the idea-generation ("brainstorming") phase. The objective here is to generate as many ideas as possible, not to decide on their merits.

b. All ideas are encouraged. No idea is too "crazy" to mention. Creativity is the goal, and members are encouraged to say whatever occurs to them as a solution, no matter how far-fetched it may seem. Far-fetched ideas may trigger more practical ones.

c. Quantity is more important than quality at this stage. The more ideas there are, the more likely it is that there will be several useful ideas.

d. "Piggybacking" is encouraged. Members should feel free to combine ideas and to add to or build on the ideas of others in order to create combinations, improvements, or variations.

The Evaluation and Selection Phase

1. It should be clear whether this group will make the final decision on the solution or will make recommendations only.

2. Criteria are established by which the ideas will be evaluated. The criteria may include feasibility, complexity, cost, human factors, timing, quality, resources required, safety, work flow, and any other pertinent factors. It should be decided whether any idea must meet a certain number of these criteria in order to be considered in the final evaluation.

3. Each idea is discussed and evaluated. Ideas may be combined.

4. It may be necessary to conduct several levels of evaluation before a final solution is selected.

5. The single idea or combination of ideas that represents the best solution is then announced to all concerned.

A New York store that specializes in lingerie has been suffering a significant decline in sales during the past year. Management is unsure about the cause(s) of this loss except that it may be attributed to more aggressive marketing by its competitors (large numbers of direct-mail advertisements, more ad space in the *New York Times*, more costly window displays, etc.). Because the store is unable to find additional funds for marketing, its management has decided to find new ways to increase the store's marketing efforts without spending more money.

You have been brought in as a consultant to assist in increasing the store's sales. How is this to be done?

Problems and Solutions

Goal: To allow the team members to experience a creative form of problem solving.

Group Size: Ten to twenty participants.

Time: Ten to fifteen minutes.

Materials: I. Two sheets of blank paper and a pencil for each team member.

II. An empty box, such as a shoe box, for the leader.

Setting: A room in which the participants can be seated comfortably.

Procedure: I. The leader explains that the team members are going to solve the problems that they consider to be important.

II. After giving each group member a pencil and two sheets of paper, the leader asks that each member write a problem question on one of his or her sheets of paper. The question may be personal, such as "What can be done about my family's irritability in the morning?," or it may be more political or social, such as "How can the country of India solve its problem of poverty?"

III. When the members have written their questions, the leader requests that on the second sheet of paper, each member write a solution to the chosen problem.

IV. The leader directs the members to fold their papers so that no one can read them and to place their solution sheets in a box held by the trainer. They are to keep the papers on which they have written their problem questions.

V. Each member then selects a new solution from the box. (The group members are not to look at the solutions until instructed to do so.)

VI. When all members have new solutions, the group leader solicits a volunteer to read his or her question out loud. The volunteer then unfolds the new solution and reads it aloud. For example: "The problem is 'What can be done about my family's irritability in the morning?'; the solution is 'Require them to practice family planning.'"

Adapted from S. Forbess-Greene (1983). *The Encyclopedia of Icebreakers: Structured Activities that Warm-Up, Motivate, Challenge, Acquaint and Energize.* San Diego, CA: Pfeiffer & Company.

VII. The activity continues until all members have shared their problem questions and new solutions.

Variations: I. The leader can ask that the members' problems and solutions be about work-related topics.

II. The members can exchange solutions instead of drawing them out of a box.

III. The members can be asked to place their problem questions in the box. The leader then picks a question out of the box, reads it aloud, and calls on a member to share his or her solution.

The Nominal Group Technique

Goals: I. To increase creativity and participation in team meetings involving a problem-solving and/or fact-finding task.

II. To develop or expand the team members' perceptions of critical issues within a specified problem area.

III. To obtain the input of as many individual team members as possible without the dysfunction of unbalanced participation.

Time: Two hours.

Materials: I. A copy of the Nominal Group Technique Task Form for each team member.

II. Twenty 3" x 5" index cards for each team member.

III. Blank paper and a pencil for each team member.

IV. A newsprint flip chart and several felt-tipped markers.

V. Masking tape for posting newsprint.

Setting: A room with a table and chairs for the team members. Plenty of wall space should be available for posting newsprint.

Procedure: I. The leader states that the role of everyone present is to contribute his or her perceptions, expertise, and experience to defining the critical issues within the problem at hand (in this case, the problem stated at the beginning of the Nominal Group Technique Task Form). The leader stresses that the theme of the experience is "problem centering" rather than "solution finding." After announcing that the approach to be used during this session is the "nominal group technique," the leader defines a nominal group as one in which individuals work in the presence of others but do not interact verbally with one another except at specified times.

Adapted from D.L. Ford, Jr., in J.E. Jones and J.W. Pfeiffer (Eds.) (1975). *The 1975 Annual Handbook for Group Facilitators.* San Diego, CA: Pfeiffer & Company. The version of this activity that appeared in the 1975 *Annual* was adapted from "A Team Process Model for Problem Identification and Program Planning" by A. Delbecq and A. Van de Ven, 1971, *Journal of Applied Behavioral Science,* 7, pp. 466-491. Used in this book by permission of the *Journal of Applied Behavioral Science.*

II. The leader distributes copies of the Nominal Group Technique Task Form and pencils, explains the task, clarifies that the "problem" to be addressed is printed at the beginning of the form, gives an example of the kind of response desired, and then asks the team members to complete the form. (Twenty-five to thirty minutes.)

III. After all team members have completed their task forms, the leader asks for a volunteer to record the team's ideas on newsprint and to help them clarify their ideas later. The leader then asks the team members to take turns presenting items from their forms, until no one has anything left to contribute. The leader specifies that no discussion or comment about the contributions is allowed at this time; however, the members are encouraged to contribute new ideas that are inspired by previously stated ones. As each sheet of newsprint is filled, the recorder posts it in prominent view before starting a new sheet. (Thirty minutes.)

IV. After all ideas have been exhausted, the recorder goes through all of the newsprint lists, numbering each item and leading a discussion of each so that the team members can ask questions, clarify, or elaborate where necessary and so that they can add new items if they wish. Items are not to be condensed or collapsed into categories at this point. (Fifteen minutes.)

V. Each team member is given ten 3" x 5" index cards and is asked to review all items written on the newsprint, to select the ten that he or she thinks are most critical to the solution of the problem, and to write these ten items and their corresponding numbers on 3" x 5" cards (a separate card for each item). The leader adds that after all ten cards have been completed, each team member should place the cards in front of him or her on the table, rank them from 1 to 10 in order of importance, and write each card's rank in its upper-right corner. (Fifteen minutes.)

VI. When all team members have completed the ranking task, the recorder collects the 3" x 5" cards from each member and tabulates the results on a newsprint tally sheet, which is set up as shown in the example. As each sheet of newsprint is filled, it is posted prominently before a new sheet is begun.

Item Number	Ranks Assigned by Team Members	Average of Ranks
1.		
2.		
3.		
4.		
5.		
6.		
7.		
8.		
9.		
10.		

Example of Newsprint Tally Setup

Aiming for Consensus

VII. The recorder leads a brief discussion of each item recorded during the previous step, ensuring that the team members understand what is meant by each. (Ten minutes.)

VIII. Each team member is given ten more 3" x 5" index cards and is asked to review the original newsprint list (the one generated in Steps III and IV), to select the ten items that he or she now considers most important, to write these ten items and their corresponding numbers on 3" x 5" cards (a separate card for each item), to rank them from 1 to 10 in order of importance, and to write each card's rank in its upper-right corner. The leader stipulates that this task must be completed silently and independently and that any changed opinions resulting from the previous team discussion should be reflected in the new cards. (Fifteen minutes.)

IX. Each team member is instructed to assign a value of 100 to his or her highest-priority item and a value between 0 and 100 to each of the remaining nine items to indicate relative differences in importance among the ten items. The leader specifies that each value is to be recorded immediately under the rank number in the upper-right corner of each card.

X. The recorder collects and tallies on newsprint the new rankings and the corresponding ratings.

XI. The leader leads a discussion about the entire experience, asking questions such as the following:

1. How would you describe your understanding of the issues affecting the problem before we used the nominal group technique? How would you describe your understanding of those issues now?

2. What kinds of problems that we typically face as a team might be candidates for using the nominal group technique? Which might not be?

3. What did you like about the technique? What did you dislike about it? What can you generalize about the advantages and disadvantages of the nominal group technique?

Variations: I. The leader may use the nominal group technique with a real problem that the team currently faces.

II. The leader may wish to present a problem (not necessarily the one on the task sheet), use another problem-solving technique to generate one set of responses, and then lead into this activity with a different problem. Subsequently, the team can compare the results of the two methods in terms of number of items generated, acceptance of high-priority items by all members, and so on.

Instructions: List all the facts and resources that your team will need to solve the problem stated below. Do not discuss this task with anyone; work silently and independently. If you complete the task with time to spare, please sit quietly and reconsider your list until everyone has finished and you have been given further instructions.

Problem: How would you compile and produce an informational brochure about your organization?

1. _____
2. _____
3. _____
4. _____
5. _____
6. _____
7. _____
8. _____
9. _____
10. _____
11. _____
12. _____
13. _____
14. _____
15. _____
16. _____
17. _____
18. _____
19. _____
20. _____

Communication in Problem Solving: The Shoe Store

Goals: I. To offer team members an opportunity to observe their communication patterns while they work as a team to solve a problem.

II. To allow the team members to explore interpersonal influence in problem solving.

Time: Approximately one hour.

Materials: Blank paper and a pencil for each team member.

Setting: A room in which the participants can work without interruption. Writing surfaces and comfortable chairs should be provided.

Procedure: I. The leader explains that during this activity, the members of the team will work together to solve a mathematical problem and that they must arrive at consensus. The members are urged to pay attention to how the team arrives at the conclusion so that later they can discuss the process that emerges. (Five minutes.)

II. The leader states the mathematical problem as follows:

"A man went into a shoe store and found a great bargain: a pair of shoes on sale for only twelve dollars, including tax. When he went to pay for the shoes, he handed the clerk a twenty-dollar bill. It was early in the day, and the clerk did not have any one-dollar bills. He took the twenty-dollar bill and went to the restaurant next door, where he exchanged it for twenty one-dollar bills. He then gave the customer his change. Later that morning, the restaurant owner came to the clerk and said, 'This is a counterfeit twenty-dollar bill.' The clerk apologized profusely, took back the phony bill, and gave the

Adapted from A. Zelmer, in J.W. Pfeiffer and J.E. Jones (Eds.) (1973). *A Handbook of Structured Experiences for Human Relations Training* (Vol. IV). San Diego, CA: Pfeiffer & Company.

A consensus decision is one that all team members can accept, regardless of how satisfied they are with it. Each member's opinion must be heard; no "majority-rule" voting, bargaining, or averaging is allowed.

restaurant owner two, good, ten-dollar bills. Not counting the cost of the shoes, how much money did the shoe store lose?"

III. After stating the problem, the leader distributes paper and pencils, tells the team members to begin solving the problem, and asks them to let him or her know when they have the solution.

IV. When the team members indicate that they have a solution, the leader ensures that they are all in agreement, asks for the answer ($8.00), and then asks one member to explain the process of arriving at the conclusion. (If the team members become preoccupied with the answer itself or the mathematics involved, the leader should focus their attention on the team process instead.) (Five minutes.)

V. The leader leads a discussion of the communication issues by focusing on behaviors such as the following:

1. Reacting negatively to the phrase "mathematical problem" and establishing artificial constraints;

2. Leaving the problem solving to "experts" (self-proclaimed or otherwise);

3. Adopting pressuring tactics in reaching consensus;

4. Using "teaching aids" in convincing others (scraps of paper, paper and pencil, real money);

5. Feeling distress if a wrong conclusion is reached;

6. Using listening checks and other communication-skills techniques; and

7. Refusing to set aside personal opinion in order to reach consensus.

(Twenty minutes.)

VI. The leader leads another discussion, this time focusing on the patterns of communication that were reflected in the experience, such as influence behaviors, tendencies toward one- or two-way communication modes, personal or team issues that interfered with task accomplishment, and behaviors that facilitated or hindered communication. Subsequently, the implications of these patterns for the team's future functioning are considered.

Variations: I. A ground rule may be established that the team members may use **no** teaching aids. Instead, they have to talk through the solution.

II. The leader may distribute the problem in handout form or write it on newsprint and post it on the wall.

III. The individual members may be asked to solve the problem independently prior to attending the team session.

Team Blasphemies:
Clarifying Values

Goals: I. To provide an opportunity for the team members to be creatively open about the characteristics of their team.

II. To assist the team members in identifying and comparing their values with regard to the team.

III. To allow the team members to explore the match between their own goals or values and those of the entire team.

Time: One and one-half to two hours.

Materials: I. Several sheets of blank paper and a pencil for each team member.

II. Newsprint and a felt-tipped marker.

III. Masking tape for posting newsprint.

Setting: A room with a chair and a writing surface for each participant.

Procedure: I. The leader introduces the activity by stating that it is useful for the members of a team to think from time to time about the team's objectives and whether they, as individuals, are working toward those objectives.

II. The leader explains that in the next step of the activity each team member will be writing a "team blasphemy"— a phrase or slogan so alien to what the team represents that the members will squirm in their seats when they hear it. The leader then gives examples of blasphemies for other teams:

- Accounting Department: "What difference does it make if we keep accurate records?"
- Human Resource Development (HRD) Department: "You can't teach an old dog new tricks."
- Customer Service Department: "Let the customers solve their own problems; we have our own work to attend to."
(Five minutes.)

Adapted from T. McNulty, in L.D. Goodstein and J.W. Pfeiffer (Eds.) (1983). *The 1983 Annual for Facilitators, Trainers, and Consultants*. San Diego, CA: Pfeiffer & Company.

The idea of an "organizational blasphemy" was suggested in *The Corporation Man* by Anthony Jay, Penguin Books, Ltd., 1975.

III. The team members are given blank paper and pencils and each is instructed to spend five minutes inventing a blasphemy for the team and writing this blasphemy on one of the sheets of paper. (Five minutes.)

IV. The leader calls time, collects the blasphemies, and reads them aloud while a member of the team records them on newsprint. This newsprint list remains posted throughout the activity. (Ten minutes.)

V. The team discusses the activity so far. The following topics may be included in this discussion:

1. How did it feel to consider and write down ideas of this nature?

2. Why did team members select these particular blasphemies?

3. What common themes run through the blasphemies? What might this mean in terms of the ways in which the members perceive the team?

4. What blind spots or biases in the team might these blasphemies indicate?

5. What taboos are there within the team that appear clearly in the list of blasphemies?

6. What do the blasphemies imply about the goals of the team? What do they imply about the way in which the team works?

7. Does any team member's blasphemy differ significantly from the rest? If so, what might be the reason?

8. What implications do the results of this activity have for the team? For the individual members?

(Fifteen to thirty minutes.)

VI. The leader states that blasphemies often highlight beliefs or aspects of behavior that have been "socialized out" of the team members by the team's processes. The team members then are invited to contribute their own examples of how this process of socialization has operated, if at all, within the team. (Ten minutes.)

VII. The leader states that a team is a culture within its organization's culture and that the values of these two cultures can differ to a great extent. The leader then replicates the drawing of three circles on newsprint and posts this figure prominently. The leader explains that the larger the shaded area, the more "comfortable" individuals are likely to feel in the organization or team. If the shaded area is large, the individual is confronted by less value conflict. The leader says that tension can be present whenever the individual perceives a clash between the values of one culture and the values of another culture to which it is connected (for example, personal and work or team and organization) and that these values may conflict more than one realizes.
(Five minutes.)

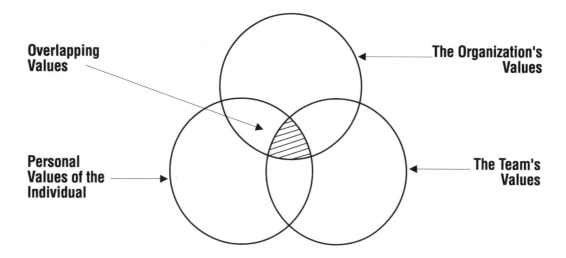

The Sets of Values That Exist Within an Organization

VIII. The leader asks the members to think about themselves in relation to the team and the organization and, using the figure of the three circles as a model, to draw circles (of approximately the same size) to represent their own values in relation to the values of their team and the values of the organization. Each member also is told to list the respective values in the three circles (his or her own values in the "personal" circle, the team's values in the "team" circle, and the organization's values in the "organization" circle). (Ten minutes.)

IX. The members are asked to take turns presenting their drawings to the total group and explaining the rationales behind these drawings. (Fifteen to thirty minutes.)

X. The leader initiates a discussion of the experience, asking questions such as the following:

1. What do the shaded areas on the drawings indicate about the match between the individual members and the team?

2. How do the team's goals match the organization's goals? How do you feel about the match? How might it affect the team? What, if anything, do you want to do about the match?

3. What values are seen as common (as shown in the shaded areas of the drawings)? What values outside the common areas are shared by individual team members?

4. How can an awareness of individual, team, and organizational values help the team members and the team in our work?

5. How can we turn the blasphemies around and state them in terms of agreed-on goals?

Variations: I. The activity can be ended after Step V.

II. The team members may be asked to complete their drawings on sheets of newsprint and post them in various places in the room. Subsequently, the members travel from "poster" to "poster" for the presentations in Step IX.

III. If the team is large, Step IX can be done in pairs.

Chapter 4

Directing the Process and Diagnosis

These activities can help a team to understand critical team processes such as conflict management and task delegation. Also, it will help the team to assess itself in relation to three important dimensions of teamwork:

- team member effectiveness,
- team leader effectiveness, and
- team effectiveness.

Team self-assessment is an important tool for increasing the team's effectiveness. It is the way in which the team gives feedback to itself. It helps the team learn to self-correct. When done regularly, this type of diagnosis is not threatening and helps the team to develop self-confidence and to continually improve itself.

Task Delegation: A Team Approach

Goals: I. To provide the team members with an opportunity to negotiate the delegation of tasks within the team.

   II. To increase the team members' awareness of attitudes about task delegation.

   III. To offer the team leader an opportunity to receive feedback from the team members about his or her delegation skills.

Time: A minimum of two hours and fifteen minutes; a maximum of four and one-half hours. If the team has more than eight members, the leader may want to conduct the activity in two sessions.

Materials: I. Each team member's three task lists, assigned as prework and copied onto sheets of newsprint prior to the activity:

   1. The specific tasks that the leader presently delegates to the team member;

   2. The specific tasks that the team member does not presently perform but would like to be responsible for; and

   3. The specific tasks that the team member presently has but would not mind giving up.

   II. The leader's three task lists, prepared and copied onto sheets of newsprint prior to the activity:

   1. The specific tasks that the leader presently delegates;

   2. The specific tasks that the leader presently delegates but would not mind performing himself or herself; and

   3. The specific tasks that the leader does not presently delegate but would like to.

   III. Several sheets of blank paper and a pencil for each team member, including the leader.

Adapted from T.F. Carney, in J.W. Pfeiffer and J.E. Jones (Eds.) (1981). *A Handbook of Structured Experiences for Human Relations Training* (Vol. VIII). San Diego, CA: Pfeiffer & Company.

IV. A clipboard or other portable writing surface for each team member, including the leader.

V. A newsprint flip chart and several felt-tipped markers.

VI. Masking tape for posting newsprint.

Setting: A room with movable chairs for the participants. Plenty of wall space should be available for posting newsprint.

Procedure: I. After introducing the goals of the activity, the leader assists the members of the team in devising two lists: one for situations in which delegation is advisable and one for situations in which it is not. During this procedure, the leader explains his or her personal views about delegation and encourages all participants to express theirs. The leader stresses the importance of reaching consensus on the situations to be included in the lists. As final decisions are made about situations, the leader records the two lists on newsprint and posts these lists. (Thirty minutes.)

II. All members of the team, including the leader, post the newsprint lists that they prepared in advance.

III. The members are given blank paper, pencils, and clipboards or other portable writing surfaces and are asked to spend twenty minutes perusing all the lists, testing them against the lists devised in Step I, and making notes about pertinent ideas or about any clarification needed. The leader also views the lists and makes notes. (Twenty to thirty minutes.)

IV. After all members have completed their reviews, the leader leads a discussion of the contents of the lists, focusing on one member at a time. At the beginning of the discussion, the leader encourages creative thinking and reminds the members to consider each member's individual wants as well as the team's needs. During the discussion, the leader encourages the team members to ask for clarification where needed, to contribute ideas, to consider the lists of advisable and inadvisable delegation situations, and to trade or negotiate task responsibilities where appropriate. All changes in task responsibility that are agreed to are recorded on the appropriate newsprint lists; each team member is responsible for recording changes to his or her lists. (One to three hours.)

A consensus decision is one that all team members can accept regardless of how satisfied they are with it. Each member's opinion must be heard; no "majority-rule" voting, bargaining, or averaging is allowed.

V. The leader initiates a concluding discussion by asking questions such as the following:

1. How comfortable are you with the tasks that have been delegated to you?

2. How did you feel about trading and negotiating task responsibilities?

3. What have you learned about delegation?

4. What have you learned about the various attitudes toward delegation that are represented in this team?

5. How can you use what you have learned in the future?

6. When you consider my delegation habits, what would you like me to keep doing? What would you like me to do differently that would be helpful to you and or the rest of the team?

Conflict Management: Developing a Procedure

Goal: To help the team members to develop a procedure for managing conflict.

Time: Two to two and one-half hours.

Materials: I. A copy of the Conflict-Management Suggestion Sheet for each team member.

II. Blank paper and a pencil for each team member.

III. A newsprint flip chart and a felt-tipped marker.

IV. Masking tape for posting newsprint.

Setting: A room with a table and chairs for the team members. If a table is not available, the leader may substitute clipboards or other portable writing surfaces. Plenty of wall space should be available for posting newsprint.

Procedure: I. The leader distributes copies of the Conflict-Management Suggestion Sheet and asks the team members to read the sheet. (Ten minutes.)

II. The leader reviews the content of the suggestion sheet with the team members, eliciting and answering questions as necessary. (Twenty minutes.)

III. The team members are asked to select partners. Each team member is given blank paper and a pencil, and each pair of team members is instructed to write a set of guidelines for conflict management that the team can use. The leader clarifies that the ideas presented in the section of their handout entitled "A Procedure for Managing Conflict" can serve as a useful starting point and that they may approach this task in any way they wish; for example, they may borrow ideas from the handout, modify these ideas, write entirely new guidelines, or combine the handout ideas with their own. The leader stipulates that each pair of team members should be prepared to present its guidelines to the team later and to explain its reasons for including specific ideas. (Twenty to thirty minutes.)

IV. The leader asks the pairs to take turns presenting their guidelines and their reasons for choosing as they did. As this information is presented, the leader

Adapted from L. Porter, in J.W. Pfeiffer (Ed.) (1991). *The 1991 Annual: Developing Human Resources*. San Diego, CA: Pfeiffer & Company.

records it on newsprint and posts each newsprint sheet after it is filled. (Twenty to thirty minutes.)

V. The leader reviews the posted information with the team members and assists them in achieving consensus about which guidelines they want to adopt for the team.

VI. When the team members have reached consensus, the leader records the final guidelines on newsprint. Then the leader gives the newsprint list to a volunteer to reproduce and distribute to all team members. The leader also suggests posting a copy in the room in which the team usually holds its meetings.

VII. Before adjourning, the leader elicits reactions to the activity and makes concluding comments.

A consensus decision is one that all team members can accept regardless of how satisfied they are with it. Each member's opinion must be heard; no "majority-rule" voting, bargaining, or averaging is allowed.

Conflict-Management Suggestion Sheet

A Procedure for Managing Conflict

1. Do not ignore something that bothers you. Work on the issue involved before the situation becomes intolerable to you. However, if needed, a cooling-off period may be established with an agreed-on time to deal with the issue later.

2. Talk directly to the other person involved. Work with the other person to try to solve the issue yourselves.

3. If your organization has a consultant or a human resource development (HRD) specialist on staff, ask that person for suggestions on how to approach the other person or for suggestions on how to define the issue. Be sure to check back with this resource person for feedback or perspectives on the result.

4. If the solution you work out involves a potential change of work procedure, get the approval of your manager before you implement the change.

5. If someone approaches you with an issue, be willing to work on it. You also may wish to seek the help of a staff consultant or HRD person in clarifying your point of view.

6. If an individual begins to complain to you about another person who is not present, encourage that individual to talk directly with the other person instead. This approach to handling conflict is much more positive and discourages the perpetuation of rumors, false information, and so on.

7. If, after you have tried to work on the issue on your own with the other person involved—and there has been no change and the conflict still exists, ask for help from a staff consultant or HRD specialist.

Things To Keep in Mind Before Working on an Issue

1. Be sure that there is a real problem and that you are not just in a bad mood.

2. Try to identify the real issue or opportunity, not just the symptoms or personalities.

3. Be prepared to work toward a mutually agreeable solution, not just toward "winning."

4. Remember that it is all right to disagree and that the other person is not "bad" if he or she disagrees with you.

5. Keep some perspective. Relationships are not destroyed but can even be enhanced by working toward a mutually satisfactory solution to a conflict.

1. Look for a "win-win" solution—an arrangement whereby both you and the other person involved "win."

2. Do your best to put yourself in the other person's shoes.

3. Be willing to "own" part of the problem as belonging to you. (Avoid thinking "That's not my problem.")

4. Remember that talking about your feelings is more effective than acting them out.

5. Establish a common goal and stay focused on it.

6. Be persistent in coming to a satisfactory solution if it is really important to you.

7. Use the effective feedback behaviors listed below under "Giving Feedback."

8. At the end of the discussion with the other person, summarize what has been decided and who will take any next steps.

Giving Feedback

Giving "feedback" is a way of helping another person to consider changing his or her behavior. It is communication to a person that gives that person information about how he or she affects you. Used properly, it can be a helpful "guidance-control" mechanism for an individual to use in altering his or her behavior. Here are the criteria for useful feedback:

1. *It describes rather than judges.* Describe your **own** reaction. Avoid "judging" language so that the other person will feel less defensive.

2. *It is specific rather than general.* Don't say, "You are dominating." Say instead, "Just now when we were deciding the issue, you didn't listen to what I said but kept right on talking."

3. *It takes into account the needs of both the recipient and the giver of the feedback.* Feedback can be destructive when it serves only your own needs and fails to consider the needs of the other person.

4. *It is directed toward behavior that the other person can do something about.* Frustration is only increased when a person is reminded of some shortcoming over which he or she has no control.

5. *It is requested rather than "dumped."* Feedback is most useful when the recipient has asked for it.

6. *It is well timed.* In general, feedback is most useful when it occurs as soon as possible after the given behavior.

7. *It is checked to ensure that it is clear.* Ask the recipient to try to rephrase what you have said.

Leadership Style

Goals: I. To help the participants to distinguish between different styles of leadership.

II. To introduce the concept of selecting a leadership style to suit the situation.

III. To explore the difference between appropriate leadership style and authentic behavior (that is, just being yourself).

Group Size: Ten to twenty participants.

Time: One and one-half hours.

Materials: I. A copy of the Leadership Style Questionnaire for each team member.

II. A copy of the Scoring and Analysis sheet for each team member.

III. A pencil for each team member.

IV. A newsprint flip chart and felt-tipped markers.

V. Masking tape for posting newsprint.

Procedure: I. The leader introduces the activity with comments such as the following:

In this activity, we will consider the question of whether all group leaders should behave alike. Some people believe that the best leadership is provided when the leader behaves in an authentic manner, that is, the feelings and behavior of the leader are open and congruent. The belief is that it is best to be yourself. Others believe that different situations call for different leadership behaviors, even different attitudes, on the part of the leader. We are going to examine this issue and, in the process, learn more about the skills of leadership.

II. The participants are divided into groups of five or six members each. A copy of the Leadership Style Questionnaire, a copy of the Scoring and Analysis form, and a pencil are given to each member.

III. One half of the groups are directed to answer the questionnaire from the point of view of a "discussion group leader" and to write that title at the top of the questionnaire. The other half of the groups are directed to answer the

Adapted from C.R. Mill, "Situational Leadership" (1980). In *Activities for Trainers: 50 Useful Designs*. San Diego, CA: Pfeiffer & Company.

questionnaire from the point of view of a "director of a task force" and to write that title at the top of the questionnaire.

IV. The leader announces that the members will have forty minutes in which to answer the questionnaire, score it, and discuss the results within their small groups.

V. The leader may want to offer assistance to individual members to see that the scoring is done properly.

VI. The entire group is reassembled for a discussion of the following questions:

1. If any of the members achieved a "perfect" score, did those individuals feel that some of their answers called for unauthentic behaviors?

2. In what way did members of the group differ in their interpretations or acceptance of the answers?

VII. Using group members' contributions, the leader lists on newsprint the goals of a group discussion leader and those of a task force director. Then the leader asks the members to determine whether different behaviors might be necessary to achieve these goals.

VIII. The leader asks the members to identify some skills that they still need to develop in order to be versatile leaders.

You are the leader of a _____

Instructions: There are ten situations described in this questionnaire. Each situation has three alternative actions listed; they are possible attitudes or positions that you might have as the group leader or director. Read each of the alternative statements and rank them in the following manner:

Write 3 next to the position you would be **most likely** to take on the statement.

Write 2 next to the position you would be **next most likely** to take on the statement.

Write 1 next to the position you would be **least likely** to take on the statement.

1. The leader of a meeting should:

_____ (1) Focus attention on the agenda (either written or hidden).

_____ (2) Focus attention on each person's feelings, in order to help the members to express their emotional reactions to the issue.

_____ (3) Focus attention on the different positions members take and the ways in which they deal with one another.

2. As a primary aim, the leader should:

_____ (4) Establish a group climate in which work and accomplishment can take place.

_____ (5) Establish a climate that encourages openness and caring.

_____ (6) Help group members to find themselves as members of the group.

3. When strong disagreement occurs between a group leader and a member, the leader should:

_____ (7) Listen to the member and try to ascertain whether the task is understood.

_____ (8) Try to get other members of the group to express themselves in order to involve them in the issue.

_____ (9) Support the person for presenting his or her views.

4. In evaluating a group's performance, the leader should:

_____ (10) Involve the whole group in assessing its learnings and satisfaction.

_____ (11) Get the group to compare its achievement with the goals it had set.

_____ (12) Allow each person to set his or her own goals and performance standards.

5. When two members of the group get into an argument, the leader should:

_____ (13) Help them deal with their feelings as a means of resolving the argument.

_____ (14) Encourage other members to help resolve it.

_____ (15) Allow some time for the expression of both sides, but keep the discussion related to the task and subject at hand.

6. The best way to motivate someone who is not performing up to his or her ability is to:

_____ (16) Point out the importance of the group's work and your need for everyone's contribution.

_____ (17) Inquire into the underlying problem in order to understand the reason for the low performance.

_____ (18) Not be concerned; the person will contribute when he or she is ready.

7. A leader's evaluation of a session should focus on:

_____ (19) The smoothness and efficiency with which the session was conducted.

_____ (20) Whether everyone contributed his or her ideas and opinions.

_____ (21) Developing a sense of achievement in both the leader and the members.

8. In dealing with hidden agendas (e.g., minority issues, low motivation), the leader should:

_____ (22) Deal openly with such issues if they threaten to disturb the relationships in the group.

_____ (23) Confront the issues quickly so that they do not divert the group.

_____ (24) Show understanding and get all the members to help deal with the issue.

9. As a goal, the leader should:

_____ (25) make sure that all the resources of group members are known and used.

_____ (26) Draw out controversy and differing opinions that may contribute to the group's goal.

_____ (27) Encourage members to contribute, if they want to do so.

10. The leader's greatest contribution to a group is to:

_____ (28) Model attitudes and behaviors that shape the group's energy.

_____ (29) Establish a climate in which true attitudes and feelings are expressed.

_____ (30) Lead subtly and allow members full opportunity to interact.

Instructions: In the columns below, next to the number of the situation, enter the number of your ranking for each action statement. Please note that the order of the numbers in the columns does not correspond with that of the questionnaire itself. In question 3, for example, the column positions are, from left to right, 7,9,8, not 7,8,9.

Situation	Action Statement	Rank	Action Statement	Rank	Action Statement	Rank
1.	(1)	___	(2)	___	(3)	___
2.	(4)	___	(5)	___	(6)	___
3.	(7)	___	(9)	___	(8)	___
4.	(11)	___	(12)	___	(10)	___
5.	(15)	___	(13)	___	(14)	___
6.	(16)	___	(17)	___	(18)	___
7.	(19)	___	(21)	___	(20)	___
8.	(23)	___	(24)	___	(22)	___
9.	(25)	___	(27)	___	(26)	___
10.	(28)	___	(29)	___	(30)	___
Total		___		___		___
		Task Force		**Feeling Oriented**		**Discussion Group**

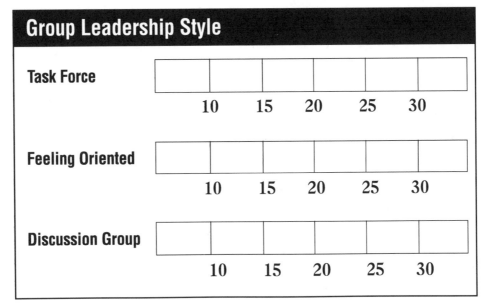

Group Leadership Style

Task Force

10　15　20　25　30

Feeling Oriented

10　15　20　25　30

Discussion Group

10　15　20　25　30

Transfer your total score for each of the columns to the bar graphs by shading the bar to the point representing your score. For comparison purposes, if you have a score of less than 30 in the type of group leadership that was assigned to you, then either your intuitive choice was erroneous for that situation or you may have a real and logical difference of opinion with the "answer." The real question is: Can you change your leadership style according to the needs of the situation?

Characteristics of Effective Team Members

Goals: I. To provide the team members with an opportunity to describe the qualities of effective team members.

II. To allow the team members to compare their own criteria for effective team members with those of other members of their team.

Group Size: Twenty or fewer participants.

Time: Twenty-five to thirty minutes.

Materials: Blank paper and a pencil for each team member.

Setting: A room with movable chairs.

Procedure: I. While distributing blank paper and pencils to the team members, the leader asks them to think about the general qualities that they believe an effective team member must possess.

II. The team members are then given three minutes to list these qualities on paper.

III. The leader asks that each member rank order the items on his or her list according to the perceived importance of each quality ("1" representing the most important quality that an employee can possess).

IV. When the members have finished their rankings, the leader asks them to divide into discussion groups of four or five members each. The members of each discussion group are to share their lists and the rationales for their selections and then attempt to reach consensus on the five most important qualities of an effective team member. (If consensus cannot be reached within nine minutes, the group members may vote to determine the group's list of qualities.)

V. After ten minutes, the leader calls the total group together and asks a volunteer from each small group to read his or her group's top five qualities aloud.

Adapted from S. Forbess-Greene, "Effective Employee" (1983). In *The Encyclopedia of Icebreakers: Structured Activities That Warm-Up, Motivate, Challenge, Acquaint and Energize.* San Diego, CA: Pfeiffer & Company.

VI. When all the discussion groups have presented their lists, the leader may process the exercise through a group discussion of the similarities and differences among the various lists. The discussion also should explore the assumptions, values, and attitudes associated with each group's selection.

Variations: I. The leader may ask the team members to rate themselves, on a scale of one to ten ("1" indicating complete competence, and "10" indicating no competence), on how they meet each of their own top five qualities.

II. After the smaller groups report on their lists, the leader may give the entire group five minutes in which to reach final consensus on the top five qualities of an effective team member.

III. After Step II, the leader may present the list that follows and ask the members if they want to add any of the characteristics to their lists.

Effective team members:

1. Support the team leader.

2. Help the team leader to succeed.

3. Ensure that all viewpoints are explored.

4. Express opinions, both for and against.

5. Compliment the team leader on team efforts.

6. Provide open, honest, and accurate information.

7. Support, protect, and defend both the team and the team leader.

8. Act in a positive and constructive manner.

9. Provide appropriate feedback.

10. Understand personal and team roles.

11. Bring problems to the team (upward feedback).

12. Accept ownership for team decisions.

13. Recognize that they each serve as a team leader.

14. Balance appropriate levels of participation.

15. Participate voluntarily.

16. Maintain confidentiality.

17. Show loyalty to the company, the team leader, and the team.

18. View criticism as an opportunity to learn.

19. State problems, along with alternative solutions/options.

20. Give praise and recognition when warranted.

21. Operate within the boundaries of team rules.

22. Confront the team leader when his or her behavior is not helping the team.

23. Share ideas freely and enthusiastically.

24. Encourage others to express their ideas fully.

25. Ask one another for opinions and listen to them.

26. Criticize ideas, not people.

27. Avoid disruptive behavior such as side conversations and inside jokes.

28. Avoid defensiveness when fellow team members disagree with their ideas.

29. Attend meetings regularly and promptly.

Items 1 through 21 by M.M. Starcevich and S.J. Stowell; Items 22 through 29 by Roger G. James and Aaron J. Elkins. Items 1 through 21 adapted from *Teamwork: We Have Met the Enemy and They Are Us* (pp. 118-119), by M.M. Starcevich and S.J. Stowell, 1990, Bartlesville, OK: The Center for Management and Organization Effectiveness. Used with permission from the publisher. Items 22 through 29 adapted from *How to Train and Lead a Quality Circle*, by R.G. James and A.J. Elkins, 1983, San Diego, CA: University Associates. The entire list may be freely reproduced for educational/training activities. *Systematic or large-scale reproduction or distribution (more than one hundred copies)—or inclusion of the items in publications for sale—may be done only with prior written permission from the respective publishers.*

Characteristics of
Effective Team Leaders

Goals: I. To provide the team members with an opportunity to describe the qualities of an effective team leader.

         II. To allow the team members to compare their own criteria for effective team members with those of other members of their team.

Group Size: Twenty or fewer participants.

Time: One-half hour to forty-five minutes.

Setting: A room with movable chairs.

Materials: I. A copy of the Effective Team Leader Sheet for each team member and for each subgroup.

         II. A pencil for each team member.

Procedure: I. The leader explains that in this activity, the members will be identifying the qualities that they believe a good team leader must possess.

         II. After giving each team member a pencil and a copy of the Effective Team Leader Sheet, the leader asks the group members, working individually, to fill out the sheets.

         III. When the team members have completed this task, the leader asks them to divide into discussion groups of four or five persons each. Next the members of each group are directed to share their individual responses with one another.

         IV. The leader gives each discussion group an Effective Team Leader Sheet and explains that each group must now complete the sheet, its members attempting to reach a consensus on the qualities that a team leader must have if he or she is to perform competently.

         V. After fifteen minutes or when the groups have completed their sheets, the leader reassembles the total group. A representative from each group then

Adapted from S. Forbess-Greene, "Good Supervisor/Manager" (1983). In *The Encyclopedia of Icebreakers: Structured Activities That Warm-Up, Motivate, Challenge, Acquaint and Energize.* San Diego, CA: Pfeiffer & Company.

reads his or her group's list of characteristics to the entire group. The leader records the characteristics on newsprint, placing a star next to those that are described by more than one subgroup.

VI. The leader then leads the members in forming clusters or categories of listed characteristics and labeling these categories (e.g., "leadership," "scheduling," "fairness," "knowledge of the task," etc.).

VII. The leader initiates a discussion of how leadership characteristics affect the team and its work.

Variations:

I. The leader may have the team members focus on the qualities of poor team leadership. (The handout would need to be modified accordingly.)

II. The leader may ask the team members to share specific examples that illustrate the characteristics of the effective team leader.

III. After Step II, the leader may present the list entitled "Characteristics of Effective Team Leaders" and ask the members if they want to add any of the characteristics to their lists.

1. An effective team leader has the following qualities:

a.

b.

c.

d.

e.

2. An effective team leader expects his or her team members to:

a.

b.

c.

d.

e.

3. An effective team leader never:

a.

b.

c.

d.

e.

Effective team leaders:

1. Communicate.

2. Are open, honest, and fair.

3. Make decisions with input from others.

4. Act consistently.

5. Give the team members the information they need to do their jobs.

6. Set goals and emphasize them.

7. Keep focused through follow-up.

8. Listen to feedback and ask questions.

9. Show loyalty to the company and to the team members.

10. Create an atmosphere of growth.

11. Have wide visibility.

12. Give praise and recognition.

13. Criticize constructively and address problems.

14. Develop plans.

15. Share their mission and goals.

16. Display tolerance and flexibility.

17. Demonstrate assertiveness.

18. Exhibit a willingness to change.

19. Treat team members with respect.

20. Make themselves available and accessible.

21. Want to take charge.

22. Accept ownership for team decisions.

23. Set guidelines for how team members are to treat one another.

24. Represent the team and fight a "good fight" when appropriate.

By M.M. Starcevich and S.J. Stowell. Adapted from *Teamwork: We Have Met the Enemy and They Are Us*, by M.M. Starcevich and S.J. Stowell, 1990, Bartlesville, OK: The Center for Management and Organization Effectiveness. Used with permission of the publisher. This entire list may be freely reproduced for educational/training activities. *Systematic or large-scale reproduction or distribution (more than one hundred copies)—or inclusion of this list in publications for sale—may be done only with prior written permission from The Center for Management and Organization Effectiveness.*

Evaluating Team Effectiveness

Periodically, the team should examine its processes from task and maintenance aspects. In doing this, the team examines how well it is doing and what, if anything, may be hindering its operation. Effective evaluation is probably one of the most critical factors in team development.

The team evaluations that follow can be used as observational tools by an independent observer or as intervention devices for the entire team. For team critiques, an assessment should be completed by each team member, who will then share his or her assessment with the entire team. Agreement about areas of improvement then lead to action planning.

Effective Team-Member Assessment

For each statement, refer to the following scale and determine your level of agreement with the statement, using the appropriate number.

Strongly Disagree	Disagree	Do Not Know	Agree	Strongly Agree
1	2	3	4	5

_____ 1. Team members ask questions to test their own understanding.

_____ 2. Team members participate in setting goals for the team.

_____ 3. Team members help the leader to track and evaluate progress toward goals.

_____ 4. Team members contribute ideas from their own experiences and knowledge.

_____ 5. Team members listen to the other members.

_____ 6. Team members build on other members' ideas.

_____ 7. Team members consider other members' ideas.

_____ 8. Team members ask questions.

_____ 9. Team members think creatively.

_____ 10. Team members focus on common interests and goals.

_____ 11. Team members make their own needs known.

_____ 12. Team members disagree in a constructive way.

_____ 13. Team members keep the purpose of the meeting in mind.

_____ 14. Team members stay focused on the objectives.

_____ 15. Team members use their own energy and enthusiasm to help the process along.

Created by Fran Rees.

Effective Team-Leader Assessment

For each statement, refer to the following scale and determine your level of agreement with the statement, using the appropriate number.

Strongly Disagree	Disagree	Do Not Know	Agree	Strongly Agree
1	2	3	4	5

_____ 1. Team leader sets boundaries.

_____ 2. Team leader interprets company goals.

_____ 3. Team leader facilitates the team's setting of its own goals.

_____ 4. Team leader evaluates and tracks progress toward goals.

_____ 5. Team leader asks questions.

_____ 6. Team leader listens effectively.

_____ 7. Team leader shows understanding.

_____ 8. Team leader summarizes discussions.

_____ 9. Team leader seeks divergent viewpoints.

_____ 10. Team leader records ideas.

_____ 11. Team leader uses group-process techniques.

_____ 12. Team leader seeks common interests.

_____ 13. Team leader confronts in a constructive way.

_____ 14. Team leader gives clear directions.

_____ 15. Team leader intervenes to keep the group on track.

_____ 16. Team leader reads the group and makes appropriate adjustments.

_____ 17. Team leader suggests alternative processes to help group achieve goal.

---

[1] Created by Fran Rees.

Effective Team Assessment

Instructions: Rate your team on each of the following nine dimensions, using a scale of one to seven, to indicate your assessment of your team and the way it functions. Circle the number on each scale that you feel is most descriptive of your team.

1. Goals and Objectives

1	2	3	4	5	6	7

There is a lack of commonly understood goals and objectives.

The team members understand and agree on goals and objectives.

2. Utilization of Resources

1	2	3	4	5	6	7

All resources of team members are not fully recognized and/or utilized.

The resources of all team members are fully recognized and utilized.

3. Trust and Conflict Resolution

1	2	3	4	5	6	7

There is little trust among team members, and conflict is evident.

There is a high degree of trust among team members, and conflict is dealt with openly and worked through.

Reprinted from M. Alexander, "The Team-Effectiveness Critique," in L.D. Goodstein and J.W. Pfeiffer (Eds.) (1985). *The 1985 Annual: Developing Human Resources*. San Diego, CA: Pfeiffer & Company.

4. Leadership

1	2	3	4	5	6	7

One person dominates, and team-leadership roles are not carried out or shared.

There is full participation in leadership; leadership roles are shared by team members.

5. Control and Procedures

1	2	3	4	5	6	7

There is little control, and there is a lack of procedures to guide team functioning.

There are effective procedures to guide team functioning; team members support these procedures and regulate themselves.

6. Interpersonal Communications

1	2	3	4	5	6	7

Communications between team members are closed and guarded.

Communications between team members are open and participative.

7. Problem Solving / Decision Making

1	2	3	4	5	6	7

The team has no agreed-on approaches to problem solving and decision making.

The team has well-established and agreed-on approaches to problem solving and decision making.

8. Experimentation / Creativity

1	2	3	4	5	6	7

The team is rigid and does not experiment with how things are done.

The team experiments with different ways of doing things and is creative in its approach.

Directing the Process and Diagnosis

9. Evaluation

1	2	3	4	5	6	7

The team never evaluates
its functioning or process.

The team often evaluates
its functioning and process.

References and Bibliography

Forbes-Greene, S. (1983). *The encyclopedia of icebreakers: Structured activities that warm-up, motivate, challenge, acquaint and energize.* San Diego, CA: Pfeiffer & Company.

Francis, D., & Young, D. (1979). *Improving work groups: A practical manual for team building.* San Diego, CA: Pfeiffer & Company.

Pfeiffer, J.W. (Ed.). (1989). *The encyclopedia of group activities: 150 practical designs for successful facilitating.* San Diego, CA: Pfeiffer & Company.

Pfeiffer, J.W. (Ed.), & Ballew, A.C. (Assoc. Ed.). (1991). *Theories and models in applied behavioral science* (Vol. 3, Management/Leadership). San Diego, CA: Pfeiffer & Company.

Pfeiffer, J.W. (Ed.), & Nolde, C. (Assoc. Ed.). (1991). *The encyclopedia of team-development activities.* San Diego, CA: Pfeiffer & Company.

Pfeiffer, J.W., & Jones, J.E. (Eds.). (1969-1985). *The handbooks of structured experiences for human relations training* (Vols. I–X). San Diego, CA: Pfeiffer & Company.

Pfeiffer, J.W., & Jones, J.E./Goodstein, L.D. (Eds.). (1972-1992). *The annual handbook for group facilitators/The annual for facilitators, trainers, and consultants/The annual: developing human resources.* San Diego, CA: Pfeiffer & Company.

Rees, F. (1991). *How to LEAD work teams.* San Diego, CA: Pfeiffer & Company.

Schindler-Rainman, E., Lippitt, R., & Cole, J. (1988). *Taking your meetings out of the doldrums* (rev. ed.). San Diego, CA: Pfeiffer & Company.